"I made myself from all the love you no longer wanted."
–Iain S. Thomas, *iwrotethisforyou*

Bittersweet

Cover & Illustrations by Zach Holt.

rubbish

When you tell them all about me
don't you dare say you lost me
because you know
damn well

you threw me away.

The problem with being a writer is
we want to be the authors of our own lives.
We want to write all the plot twists and the happy endings and the sad parts that turn into
hopelessly romantic paragraphs,
but we can't.
We cannot be the authors of our own lives
because our lives are novels
that have no authors,
only editors.

The truth is that disagreements within a relationship are inevitable. Whether it be over a cup of coffee spilled on your English report, or spending too much money on clothes or a new video game instead of helping to pay rent.
The truth is that at the end of the day, the arguments and bickering get set aside when you're sleeping next to the one you love. This is a high level of vulnerability and trusting unconscious presence in the hands of each other.
And that is more important than paying a little extra money for rent, or not buying your weekly almond milk.
But, when it comes down to only one person thinking that way is when everything starts to lose its meaning. Sleeping next to them starts to become a habit versus something to look forward to. It starts to feel routined, rather than comforting, like the way you drive to work every day or always take a shower after the gym.
The truth is, conflicts in a relationship are inevitable, but they can always be resolved. Compromise is possible. If love has been deteriorating over time, simply looking into your partner's eyes before they fall asleep can even start to lose its significance.

The truth is, I kept fighting as you pushed me further and further away, because my love had not burned out and I still believed in solutions. I fought until you pushed me so far that I became lost, unable to find any reason to keep fighting.
So don't blame me for being the one who caused us to become distant due to fights and arguments, because darling, I always forgot about every one of them as I lay beside you at the end of the day.
The sad truth is, you were able to make me smile my big cheesy smile, hear my giggly laugh during tickle fights, look into my sleepy eyes under your chin, feel my gentle hands caress your cold heart, listen to me whisper one last "I love you" in your ear,
and three days later,
you were still able to say
"I don't want this, anymore."

ripped library card

Thank you for returning to me
like an old favorite book.
It made me realize that
I don't want to read this book
anymore.

half-loved

I'd rather be alone for the rest of my life than only half-loved by you.

Getting to know a new person is like moving to a new country. You don't know the roads, the street signs, the sweet spots, or the "bad sides of town." Hell, you don't even know the typical climate or how the weather changes in that area.

Now, I have never moved to a new country, I've been living in the same place for my entire nineteen-and-a-half years, but I have only known one home.

After three years of being in this home, I knew the traces of his skin. I knew where all his funny freckles were. I knew about the tattoo on his ass he got when he was sixteen. I knew the changes in his tone of voice and what emotions they represented. I knew the looks on his face when he felt any kind of feeling

(because, darling, we could speak without saying a single word).

I knew how to make him sigh sweet exhales of exhaustion.

I knew how to stray away from the "bad sides of town,"

and I knew all the sweet spots and how to keep them at bay.

I had memorized the entire topography of his being.

--Or, at least I thought so.

No matter how strong or how weak, at some point a storm comes and does some damage.

There can be easy repairs—

or some that take a little extra work to get back to a beautiful,

sturdy home.

This happened with us, of course. We had some bricks that fell off our chimney and a few loose floorboards, but we always fixed them or made them sturdy enough to work.

I guess what's killing me is that I never saw this past storm coming.

It was a hurricane, and I thought we had built a strong enough foundation to last through it.

I guess what's killing me the most is that I was wrong.

for $2.89 x 5

Any time I start to miss you,
I just think about how after three years of all of the unconditional love I gave you,
After three years of everything I've done to help you,
on that night when I had a complete breakdown
and my parents had to hold me down from throwing furniture into the walls,
hide my prescription meds,
And I was on the floor
shaking
I was on the floor
numb
All I asked for was you to come get me,
And you said you only would if I gave you gas money.

fire

I knew I was playing with fire as I reached for his hand.
Now, I can't tell whether I should start preparing myself to burn or ignite.

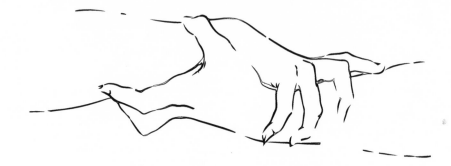

(spoken) on being

You know what? So what if I love like a main lead role from a Shakespeare play? So what if
my efforts of affection appear to be those of a Elizabethan hopeless romantic?

Hell yeah, I write love letters. I don't care if I see you every day or once a month,
you're getting some damn heartfelt letters.

So what if I write poems about you after only knowing you for a short period of time? Am
I wrong to be sensitive? Shit, I don't care if I've never spoken to you—
if I find you attractive and fall in love with you for even a brief glance,
you better expect at least three-to-four stanzas of a poem written about how I'll always long
to know you.

So what if I want to be wooed on the first or second date? Should I want anything less?
While you ask me the (quite frankly—annoying) basics of the awful interview, yes, I'll be
imagining us having it in the middle of a city, on a chilly night, dancing to Ol' Blue Eyes in
the center of an empty street. Maybe I'll even get swung off my feet and into a heart-melting
kiss. Yes, I'll be fantasizing about having a first date like Noah and Allie.[1]

So what if I want an experience of a first date that is similar to one in the novels I adore or
my old fashioned Audrey movies? So what if I say or do little things that hint that I want to
dance or run around the city? At least I have character.
I'm tired of feeling like I need to be less affectionate and more cool. Cool Girl. I can't be
Cool Girl. I feel like I need to be constantly holding up a solid shield that blocks me from
my natural sensitivity.

Sure, I have high standards at this point in my life
but, don't we all?
Why should that reflect on me as a person?

"Emma, Can you just chill out?"

No, damn it. If you broke my heart or if you awed me, yeah, for fucks sake I'll be expecting
some National Book Award worthy novel of an apology or a longing for my heart.
Why is being a hopeless romantic viewed so terribly? We make the best lovers and friends.
We make those novels for you all to read and enjoy. We make those movies for you to cry
over. We are the creators of indecisive romance. We are the producers of comfort poetry. We
writers help expose the feelings for those who are lost, confused, found, in love, out of love,
searching for help, looking for survival, or even just a smile.
So, so damn what if I like to think I'm living in the 50s with a heart of a romantic Elizabethan?
It made me able to write this.

1. Reference to *The Notebook* by Nicholas Sparks

ghosts

You left
so please

leave

write about loss and beauty

And somehow the loss made everything that wasn't,

beautiful.

something he picked up in europe

Pain is only predicted when it's self-inflicted.
How sweet it would be to foresee
A heartbreak, a headache, or even an earthquake.

They say that an unexpected storm
is necessary to grow and transform
into a flower of prosperity that blooms with clarity.

And yet,

Although it was just a little kiss,
all of my wounds have started with this.

one year later

I tried to forget you
But your roots wrapped around my lungs
with tangled up knots in labyrinthine places.
And the echo of your touch
pounded against my fair skin
a tattoo no one can ever see.
While your voice became the scratched vinyl
playing back and forth
on a broken record player
that won't stop skipping
And our memories flood back
submerging my hollow shell
into a place where
there seems to be no light switch.

And I kept thinking to myself,
"I am here, but you-
you are everywhere
yet nowhere."

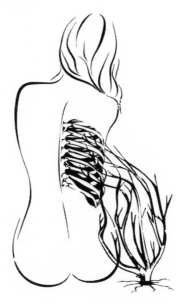

a list

In your absence
I have learned:

1. I can live without you
2. I don't want to

tide

There is a tide up along the shoreline
on the night of a full moon
it's already too far up
and it clings to the fence posts
but only for a moment
before returning to the sea.
The process continues
stronger, weaker, stronger,
but it slows down
and weakens
with each time the waves
roll back into themselves
and find their
whole.

And this is what falling out of love feels like.

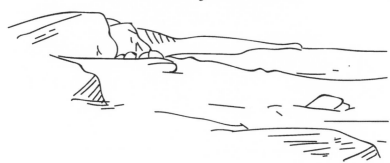

infatuation

You are everything I never thought I'd want
and now I am on the edge of
confusing love with infatuation.

She likes her coffee dark
and her appearance bright
so no one can see
all of her disheveled misery.

white flags

Taking drugs that alter your mental state
over a period of time
is a war between:

self-care
vs.
suicide

happy pills or pills?

I'm not sure which is more sad:
Being put on medication for not being happy
or
asking to take the pills away
out of the fear
of them working.

waiting

I walked out the door with your touch echoing upon my skin,
And I'm still waiting for you to kiss me.

She always walks around with the biggest smile on her face. Her porcelain skin glistens as it curls on the corners of her mouth and scrunches in the center of her nose when she laughs. One would look at her and think, "Unique."
Her smile comes off as a glowing happiness when she says hello to strangers and when she always tells the cashier to "Have a great day," as she makes purchases. Her eyes are soft, green, always looking, and never stop looking
innocently curious.
She treats everyone with kindness, no matter how they wrong her. She aims to be the sunshine people can see if they are facing rain. She tries to come off as being happy, fun, and carefree.
She is also an impeccable actress.
There is a certain sorrow in her eyes that most do not notice at their first or second glance at her. She is very good at hiding it by this point, she's been practicing.
She wanted to be the author of her own life.
Daydreaming was a profession for her—
always trying to plan the plot twists, the good parts, and the bad parts of her life.
She regularly fantasized of men coming up to her like in the romance novels that she loves (so much).
All she ever wanted was to love and be loved. She put together scenes of men treating her sweeter than Tupelo honey—
A dream that seems only to be fantasy.
She wears her heart on her sleeve because the first thing everyone notices is what she is wearing.
There is a sadness behind her crooked smile that she flashes ever so frequently. There's a numbness hiding behind the way she carries herself (featherlight and gracefully clumsy). Although she dances on her own frequently without a care in the world who is watching, there's a certain emptiness that follows her actions when she wishes to herself that she had someone to dance with.
She sits quietly in corners, reading books, and over-thinking.
Wondering who could be watching her and wondering if maybe perhaps maybe— they are who thought of this.

- an excerpt of myself through the eyes of someone
i'll never meet

You fell in love with my petals
But not with my roots

So when they begged for warmth
You forgot to place me on a new sill
where the sunlight would shine through at
a different time for refill

And when my soil became dry
You forgot I needed water
from a spout held by your hands
it may as well have been slaughter

You fell in love with my petals
But you forgot to nurture my roots
with your hands and your words
all you did was convolute

And I am so much more
Than a mere convenience.

Picking up my old favorite book,
I searched for my favorite underlined quotes and
flipped the pages to the specific ones that I "dog-eared"
to remember.
Then I decided to read the parts in between the folds,
once more.
The parts that were not significant to me upon the first time reading.
I read them again and remembered why I never left a marker:
Flowers once so delicately pressed among pages (tattered from the start) had gone pale
and dry,
And there is nothing nostalgic about oppression.
I decided to count
how many pages were flagged over the years
for blissful reminiscence
Only to find that I had more fingers on my fragile hands that once held this book so
dearly,
Than memories
that were once meaningful
out of a three-part novel.
Chuckling to myself,
I let out a sigh as I gently closed the book and placed it not back on my beloved shelf,
but in the back of the armoire
to sit aside other forgotten promises.

sweetly hollow

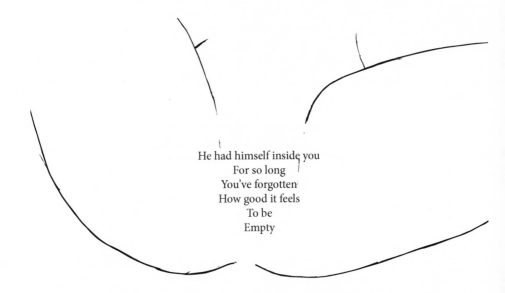

He had himself inside you
For so long
You've forgotten
How good it feels
To be
Empty

hear no see no speak no

If actions speak louder than words, how is it you were able to convince me that you don't love me anymore when you were softly kissing me once more? How were you able to convince me that you didn't need me anymore when you were caressing my body in all of the familiar places? How is it that you were able to convince me that you didn't want me anymore, when you were deep inside me, moaning, grasping my waist and engraving your fingers into my skin?
Because actions don't speak louder than words.

You were able to open me back up like your favorite old book.
You took me off your shelf and blew my dust off.
Cracked my spine open to a place where you could pick right back up and still remember every:
line, quote, sentence structure,
funny way the printer messed up,
and
then you were able to put me back on the shelf
without reading another word.

You haven't said anything to me in weeks days
and there is nothing more deafening than silence.

"You're too: sensitive,

quirky, clumsy, shy, nice, cute,
introverted, affectionate, small, "weird", intimidating,
romantic.

I wish you could be more: outgoing,

spontaneous, sexy, happy, open-minded,
extroverted, colorful, adventurous,
easy-going."

And I guess that's what scares me the most:
being too much,
and at the same time,
not enough.

after or over coffee?

Tell me what pushes your buttons
while I undo mine.

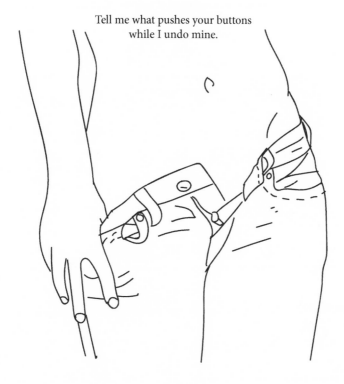

1545

When I walk into an old mailroom
that still has the little boxes with the locks you turn and twist
or the kind with certain keys
I think about the vintage stories that rest within them
from many years before.
How many others have come to this post office:
during the times of war,
depression, boomers.
How many others came to this mail room
in hopes of a letter that would give them joy
only to find their hearts shattered.
And who has shared my same letterbox
From all the years before?
Who has found the same triumphs as I
inside this little box?
Or did they find something
that tore their world apart?
When I see these antique mailrooms,
I don't wonder what I may find,
but rather what have others found
in my same place?
And how many have come back to their letterbox,
only to find it empty —
yet again.

closed doors

        In a time of confusion--my eyes swirling around a kaleidoscope of indecisiveness, and my body at a standstill within a hallway of a manifold of curious doors. It was a time where I could point to any spot on my pale flesh and have something negative to say. And the very first insignificant boy I fell in love with emphatically stressed my need to change my disposition. *"Dear, you need to be less this and more that,"* he'd say. *"Darling, I don't understand why you want to change me,"* I'd say. *"I don't want to change you, I just wish you'd do this more and that less,"* he'd say. *"Okay,"* I'd say.
        It's been one year now since he's left because I didn't conform to his ideal lover. And although I'm still standing in the same hallway, it's become a little smaller since I shut that door and left a hanger on it that reads, *"Do Not Disturb."*

moving on

She used to submit to his every need
As if a vase could not be left
unfilled.

Now that he has been walking a lonesome pavement
empty of color
for some time
he has begun to pick flowers
that aren't there
and will never again
grow.

You know that same story you've heard numerous times? Girl meets boy, girl falls in love, boy breaks her heart. Yeah, those. It's interesting that sort of timeline has been a steady repetition told at many family gatherings, girls night outs, and late-night telephone conversations and yet, the last part of that stream of events is always unpredictable. Or, perhaps it is predictable and we set ourselves up to have our hearts broken anyways. But I suppose that's what we have to do, otherwise we would have to force ourselves to go numb and never feel again. And who wants that? It's better to feel something than nothing at all.

i still think about you all the time

Will he leave her head?
The answer is no.
All she wants is him
and to never let go.

to a boy who made me cry

When I was put on medication
A year ago to-day
"It won't make you numb,"
They said, *"but will keep the pain at bay."*

Yet, after this I felt solid,
Whole and cold as a stone.
As if concrete had filled my lungs
And ice coated my bones.

Afraid the doctors lied to me,
I tried to find someone near.
A boy who could make me smile,
Or even shed a tear.

I searched and searched for much too long
Until I could no longer cope;
It was then that I found you, dear,
Offering all different kinds of hope.

But then you changed and became
Cruel, like all the rest.
Taking back every word you said,
And ripping my heart from its chest.

I was sad for awhile,
And cried until I couldn't
But then I gave a chuckle
Because I realized that I shouldn't.

You made me realize that I'm not numb,
And you are just an ass.

but you don't give a second thought about me

In the morning time
and in the evening, I dream;
It's always of you.

never felt more alone

She longs to be empathized;
For someone to listen,
And even attempt to make sense
at her bouquet of clumsy words
That stutter like the scratched record
Hidden under her shelf.

The unnoticed wallflower,
Craves her hand to be taken
Rather than cupping her mouth,
Trying to be noticed
in a room so full.

She is unable to hear herself
screaming
In such a crowded place,
and yet,
only a few may flinch.

"Probably just the wind."

we were over before we started

> They never understood us
> —but,
> that's okay.
> I don't think
> we ever really understood,
> either.

perhaps you were the danger rather than the safety

I've not felt so safe,
Since you took me by the hand.
Why did you let go?

magnetics

I whisper, *"love*
why would our
symphony fiddle with time?"

but her blood will have
rose from your moan
like the bitter soul
it lies in.

but you're with her

I long to hold you;
Kiss away your loneliness.
It is you, I dream.

impatience

Although she felt an extraordinary love awaited her,
She was impatient as the days passed.
And in her solitude
She was sorrowfully pensive

nothing more.

lonely

There are a lot of lonely words to say,
But the loneliest of all is, "stay."

show me every shameful bruise

Tell me your stories,
your aspirations and fears;
I will still love you.

You know that place in between dreaming and waking?

Meet me there.

Together we can pretend
that anything is possible.
And maybe while we're there,
we can facilitate a place
where you are mine,
and I am yours.

Meet me there.

Dear Heart, Dearest Brain,

Listen here, this is key
No matter how much you worry,
if it's meant to be, it will be

poison

But when will your name
Stop feeling like poison
That singes my tongue
and leaves these stained lips
burned?

if you're a mess, I'm messier

And that's when I realized,
it's okay to love someone
and not want to spend
the rest of your life with them.
Imagine all the things that drove you nuts
and dealing with them every day.
This allows you to find someone whose mess
becomes your mess too
and you're okay with that.

We loved each other, that's for sure.
But, we knew we would never make it.

alone

And all the while she longs to be held,
She knows she did it to herself
By pushing away those who loved her
out of fear that they would leave.
And although she craves to be kissed,
she blames herself the culprit
of her own sorrows.
Placing herself into the darkness
She endeavored to avoid.
Her curiously innocent eyes wander,
searching for a hand to hold
While inside she is screaming
For compelling herself into being
what she fears most.

Denial

Withdrawing her pen,
She will not write about him,
Realizing it's love.

I wrote a poem
or two
about you
when I thought we were over.

It's not until now
That I realized how
When you are really through,
You can't write one
or two,
or three,
If you're never meant to be.

Even if you've come a long way,
You'll find there are no words left to say.

As the pills were cut in half,
her less than frequent smiles
were simultaneously divided.

How sadly beautiful that her moderate happiness
was nothing but a mask
of orange bottles.

She knew what she needed to be happy,
anyway.
And that was something that no medication could
ever give her.

questions and answers

Rather than asking me about myself,
ask me about my favorite book
and you will learn
all you need to know.

sugar & spice

And much like cinnamon,
I am both bitter
and sweet.
You crave my taste,
but too much of me
and you will choke.

foolish

Do you think maybe there is some larger than life reason
why we continue to find ourselves in each other's arms once more?
Even after all the times we have shoved them away?
Are the moon and sun collaborating to bring us together?
-- Or are we
(or am I)
just foolish?

gentle reminder

He became my other half,
when I really needed someone to remind me:
it's okay to not be whole.

i'll show you mine if you show me yours

Show me all your scars,
Tell every aching story,
I'll love you anyways.

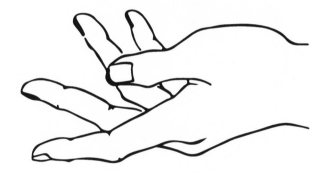

How is it possible that I want him so much, yet yearn to keep my Independence?
Becoming too close means Dependency is lingering, walking hand in hand with
Vulnerability and bringing weakness to the blood, flowing throughout your body.
"Don't let your guard down," Conscious says.
"But, I want him," I respond.
"Are you willing to risk another heartbreak?
You remember what happened last time," Conscious says.

Keeping the detachment can be significant.
It helps separate the differences between wanting him for him
or the idea of having him.

Finding that I want him, I replied to Conscious,
"Yes."

game changer

It wasn't until I met you that I learned the difference
between loving and being in love.

You can fall in and out of love for someone,
but loving,
that's permanent.

Sunflower Girl

Sunflower girl with her hair in a bob
That blushes her cheeks with a warm caress
Wearing her yellow 1960s dress
She keeps to herself, like a locked doorknob.

Sunflower girl wears her heart on her sleeve
And unintentionally has her chest in a knot
With a certain sorrow she can't seem to spot
Thinking to herself, *"Why do they all leave?"*

Sunflower girl with her head in the clouds
Dreaming of men whom she may never know
Wondering how to find them; where to go
And why her charm couldn't be endowed.

Although radiant in the summer wind,
She is more elegant during the fall
Ravishing in any season that comes,
She is bright even when she can't stand tall.

She waits patiently to be chosen,
In a field of others with sweet traits shared
As the only sunflower unaware
of her incomparable uniqueness.

i can't get you out of my head

At sunrise, I wake;
Thoughts of you invade my mind;
They stay there all day.

another poem about you

Darling, don't you see?
I will love you for your flaws.
You are safe with me.

nana

And although you left me too soon,
I only hope that wherever you are,
there is both wine
and a cat
because you and I both know
that's all you need
to be happy.

clouds

How ironic that you're able to bring my head down
from out of the clouds
When you're the one who put it there.

aa

I never lived in a sheltered household, but rather one that hushed up about the less than average mental struggles held within our family. It wasn't until a class at school introduced me to a recovered alcoholic, that I had my first real exposure to what can happen to those who let unavoidable genetics in.

As he stood there, I noticed his hands uncontrollably shaking.
I wondered if it was his older age, Parkinson's, perhaps?
Until, he revealed that he was only in his mid-sixties
And that chronic disease was not the cause
Of his beyond aged skin,
Or trembling limbs.
He paced back and forth,
Walking on a limp,
And appeared to stomp
With every step,
Rather than heel-to-toe.
And as he began his story,
The class went silent.

"You see," he said,
"I was born into this life. "
Alcohol addiction within his family co-worked with emotional abuse.
He continued a tale of no ups, only downs,
Of how he struggled with addiction
And
never
wished
To change.
In and out of rehab,
The man could not find
Motivation
Or happiness
Anywhere,

Except at the bottom of a bottle.
Or eight.
Or ten.
"Until one day," he said,
"I knew I was going to go insane,
Death is inviting
Insanity is not.
I knew I would rather die than go insane,
Because once you go insane - really insane,
No one can save you,"
"Right now," he said, *"I can be saved."*

Which led him to another center for rehab where he stayed for months and even longer
after they felt he was good to go. He chose to stay to save himself. I won't forget when he
looked at the class and said, *"For the first time in over sixty years, I'm happy to be alive."*
Wiping the tears from my eyes, I was glad to hear his words. Because only being aware of
textbook-style hyperbolized stories is nothing compared to real ones.

I pitied him at first,
But then I realized
To be excited for him
And all of his unexplored opportunities
He has yet to discover.
And will do so,
With a hell of a survival story
To make each and every new moment
Exceedingly precious.

And I'll remember him
That nameless man with the shaking hands
As someone who was eager
To greet the life that had passed him
Throughout so many years before
As an old friend
With a handshake that is just as
unsteady, but strong
As he is.

hopeless romantic

She is poetry
Her language is spoken song
Of longing for love.

bittersweet

Come to me in all of your disheveled sorrows
And with that the weight of every burden
Oppressing your already tender heart;
I will not let go of your hand.

Come to me in all of your exhaustion,
From using every last bit of strength
To hold your head high,
Here, you may rest.

Come to me in all of your remorse,
Show every shameful bruise that blackens your skin;
I will turn on a light to show you
That your silhouette is still the most beautiful.

There's no need to run when you feel your heartbeat.
My dear, loving you has been bittersweet.

darling, why don't you see me

In the morning light
I covet to be with you
And still, when it fades.

eclipse

you wrote about my *"moonless midnight hair"*
but you forgot to mention the moon in my eyes
or the stars in my laugh
and how the glistening planets have composed
me into living by my own intuition
and not needing any of your sun.

October

November days
drawing near;
It's cold outside,
I need you here.

breathless

I find myself only able to write
The shortest of words about you;

maybe that's because
you leave me breathless.

lights

Have you ever seen those gadgets for long distance relationships?
The kind where you can touch an object and the one your partner has will light up?
I love that idea.

Coming home to find the light on,
I touch mine to hold your hand
even though you're not there.
We could see the fire we start,
and the light we create
will burn the distance
and bring you to me.

summer days

She longs for those warm summer days,
dancing in strawberry fields where
beneath her dress, she's wet with pleasure
from the soft winds blowing gentle kisses
where she has on no panties.

you may let your guard down

Rest your heart with me.
Darling love, I swear to you,
I will keep it safe.

winter

Although she craves
the gentle heat of
those favorable
summer days,
There is a certain comfort
in the sorrows of winter
she just can't seem to grasp.

second best

I am not the girl men will call to see on their free nights.
I am the girl men will call when she isn't working out.

empty hands

And despite the loneliness
you've left in these empty hands,
I hope she is able to fill yours
with the most tender love
they need.

A little lady,
unbearably filled with love,
and no one to hold.

every snowfall reminds me of you

I whisper,
"I miss you,"
"I miss you,"
to the gentile snowflakes falling,
because they're falling hard
and I did, too.

playboy

"*Hmm, he looks like he'd break my heart,*"
I thought to myself.

"*I gotta have him.*"

When she was with him,
her lips tasted of a bitter-
sweet pomegranate wine,
stained with the poison
of his petulance.

Now her kisses taste like honey,
a sweetness he will never know.

candle

If a person wants to be in your life
they will make an effort to do so.
You don't need to give up every
last drop of Love your tender heart holds,
only to cry yourself dry.
So darling, don't waste your time
on someone who cannot see your flame
because they are too afraid to light the candle.

-you don't need a coward

always

In the morning time,
Or in the falling evening,
It is always you.

but you looked away

All I can remember from that day
is looking into your eyes from across your dining-room table
and thinking to myself,
"I could stay here forever."

Do you remember,
when we laid together:
my head on your chest
my hand caressing your heart?
I felt I could sink into you,
warm, slow, and deep,
so we could mold into one
and never have to leave home.

My darling, did you feel it, too?
Do you feel it, too?

echo

There is a pulsing echo of your touch
when it leaves mine.
It whispers, "Come back, come back,"
and with each and every treacherous beating,
the bruises together in unison sigh,
"Just a little longer."

recycled

I am continuously used and discarded,
reused and then regarded,
because you wanted to keep me close
and I just wonder at what point
may I be decomposed into the garden
to spread out my fingers and toes
into the soil that will forever pardon
my burdening tears.

an unbalanced thought

And she'll go on,
romanticizing men who she longs to love
and then proceeding in her actions
with continuous disappointment.

Someone once told her not to dream,
"It will cause you just as much heartache as lovers do,"
they said.

But, *"Oh well,"* she said with her chin held high.
*"I'd be rather concerned if something in my life
didn't break my heart."*

in morning light

Appearing in dreams,
It is very frustrating
To wake without you.

don't look me in the eyes

I must look away
as we stand an inch apart
or else, I'll kiss you.

emma hill

december

I can remember
(so very sweetly)
the dreamy state
of how we were
last December:

Curled up in your bed,
a storm going outside,
and a war inside my head.

'til death do us part

The ghost of you still lingers near
When you're long gone and not been here
I try to push you from my head
What we once had is now dead.

"You know how to move on quick," he said.
"Just how to apply a bandaid," she replied

it was still the most erotic

I made love,
you fucked.
I knew the difference
when your name spilled
from my mouth
and tasted like honey,
but you never once kissed me.

last night I dreamt you loved me

I never would have thought
a dream of one little kiss
could have me stuck
feeling like this.

the only attention I crave is yours

The rain falls as the sky exhales in exhaustion
and landing into a pure oblivion of fatigue
that spreads out lazily amongst the earth.

You always compared me to a rainy day
because my tears absorb into everyone around me
except you, who used an umbrella.

Where do I put all that my heart holds?
Where can I set it down?

"Well that's my problem," I said
"Once I start loving someone,
I never really stop."

counterfeit

Falling in love with love
is counterfeit art.
The mind to body connection
is where true aesthetic lies.
Beauty is only an essence
for what the mind ensnares;
The subliminal expectation you adhere
from the mere reflection of a surface
is lethargic.
And I deserve so much more than negligence.

"I don't want you to make love to me," she said,
"I want you to consume me."

choke

coward

When I looked over to see you
huddled beneath a tree
the rain was falling hard
and you couldn't stop shivering,
yet you were clutching your jacket close to you
and hanging on for dear life

just like the way
you used to hold me.

You keep your jacket close to you,
but you decide not to put it on
so although the rain gets you soaking wet,
you don't realize
you're holding your own solution.

When you reached out to me,
you asked for my hand
and when I grabbed yours
I never wanted to let go.

So, I placed my hand on your shoulder
and you looked up at me
with beautiful eyes filled with sorrow
I asked, "why don't you wear your jacket?"
to which you replied, *"I don't want to ruin it."*

So I just have to ask,
at what point did you become such a coward?

needed

She is always the one needed
At the very end of the day
For those who feel defeated
And have some things to say.

But, no one is there for her
Not a single head is raised
When she needs a gesture
To reassure her ways.

Afraid to appear conceded
And terrified of being a burden
She likes to feel needed
And at least she knows that's certain.

Acknowledgments

The biggest of thank yous to Zach Holt for his incredible illustrations and composition of this book.

Thank you to Anna for helping keep me composed throughout writing this book.

And to those who have given me consistent feedback and support throughout this process. You are the true inspiration for this little book. Thank you.

This is a book about heartbreak. This is also a book about recovering from that heartbreak and this is a product about when it happens again.. and again.. and again… This is a book about broken promises. This is a book about finding yourself amongst the broken pieces your heart was shattered into. This is a book about growth.

77725131R00061

Made in the USA
Middletown, DE
25 June 2018